Our Rainbow

Kelli Rado

This is a work of fiction. All of the characters, names, incidents, organizations, and dialogue in this novel are either the products of the author's imagination or are used fictitiously.

WestBow Press books may be ordered through booksellers or by contacting:

WestBow Press
A Division of Thomas Nelson & Zondervan
1663 Liberty Drive
Bloomington, IN 47403
www.westbowpress.com
1 (866) 928-1240

ISBN: 978-1-5127-8522-7 (sc)
ISBN: 978-1-5127-8523-4 (e)

Library of Congress Control Number: 2017906461

Print information available on the last page.

WestBow Press rev. date: 12/03/2017

WESTBOW
PRESS®
A DIVISION OF THOMAS NELSON
& ZONDERVAN

Dedicated to our angel babies.

Dearest friends,

If it was up to me, this book would never have happened. My plan was to have a baby. My plan was to be a mother. My plan fit perfectly in my life. However, life did not follow my plan. My plan was not to lose a child. My plan was not to feel such pain, heartache and loss. However, my plan isn't perfect like God's plan. Suffering is difficult, inevitable here on earth. While I may not understand why I went through this suffering, God's presence sustains me. He was with me every step of the way, drawing me closer to Him. I am so sorry for your loss and the season of grief that you experienced. My hope is for you to turn to Him for the strength, comfort, and healing that only our Lord can provide. God's plan for our lives extends beyond our own understanding; everything is perfectly crafted and will be completed on His timetable. God is good.

With love,
Kelli

"Many are the plans in a man's heart...
Proverbs 19:21

Precious Little One,

Before you arrived, Papa and Mama
were missing the one that came before.
We did not understand
what the Lord had in store.

"Consider it pure joy, my brothers, whenever
you face trials of many kinds..." James 1: 2-3

We prayed for you day and night.
We trusted God's plan was just right.

"Do not be anxious about anything...
present your requests to God." Philippians 4:6

While we waited for you, God filled
our hearts with patience, hope, and peace.
We were reminded daily
that his love for us
will never cease.

"Trust in the Lord with
all your heart..." Proverbs 3:5

When we found out you were coming,
we were over the moon!
The Lord's plan was unfolding
not a minute too soon.

"For I know the plans I have
for you..." Jeremiah 29:11

We watched in awe as
you grew week by week.
Each detail from your head
to your toes
to chubby cheeks!

"...you knit me together in my mother's womb." Psalm 139:13

Here you are! Ten fingers, ten toes.
We praise the Lord who gave you those.

"Give thanks to the Lord..." Psalm 136:1

We love you, little one.
You are our rainbow after the storm.

Love,
Papa and Mama

About the Author

Kelli Rado lives with her husband and children in Wisconsin. She is an elementary school teacher. Kelli personally has experienced the loss of a child. The Lord put this idea on her heart and she is now publishing her first book.

www.ingramcontent.com/pod-product-compliance
Ingram Content Group UK Ltd.
Pitfield, Milton Keynes, MK11 3LW, UK
UKHW062002290726
14090UKWH00021B/1350

9 781512 785227